P9-EEM-034

A
Drowning
Man
Is Never
Tall
Enough

A
Drowning
Man
Is Never
Tall
Enough

Poems by

Patrick Lawler

The University
of Georgia Press
Athens and London

© 1990 by Patrick Lawler
Published by the University of Georgia Press
Athens, Georgia 30602
All rights reserved
Designed by Betty McDaniel
Set in ten on thirteen Optima
The paper in this book meets the guidelines for
permanence and durability of the Committee on
Production Guidelines for Book Longevity of the
Council on Library Resources.

Printed in the United States of America

94 93 92 91 90   5 4 3 2 1

Library of Congress Cataloging in Publication Data

Lawler, Patrick.
    A drowning man is never tall enough :
    poems / by Patrick Lawler.
        p.   cm.
    ISBN 0-8203-1157-X (alk. paper). —
    ISBN 0-8203-1158-8 (pbk. : alk. paper)
    I. Title.
    PS3562.A867D76 1990
    813'.54—dc20   89-4823
                                    CIP

British Library Cataloging in Publication Data available

For all the support, inspiration, friendship, and love:

annbarbarabethbettybillbobcarmencatherinechrischristopher
colleendandaviddebi
donnadorisearlelinorellenemilyemmetteric
florencefrankgabrielgarygaylegengregghapharryheather
hermanjackjasonjeffreyjenniferjimjohnkarenkathykathleen
kenkevinlarrylindalisamarcelmargaretmariannemarkmartimarty
marymaureenmeghanmichellemickmikenealofeliaparkiepatrick
paulphiliprachelreginarickrobertromarosieroyryansally
seansueterriterrytheresatimtinatomvernevinnie
wallacewdwilliam
anna
janet
nicole

Contents

Acknowledgments

The author and publisher gratefully acknowledge the following
publications where these poems first appeared:

American Poetry Review: "Elagabalus, Roman Emperor, Trickster Too"
Apalachee Quarterly: "Bird by Bird"
Community Writers' Project Newsletter: "Fear"
Croton Review: "Propellers over Amsterdam"
Epoch: "Odd, the Bride Stripped Bare by Her Bachelors"
Hiram Poetry Review: "Watching the Sailboats"
Iowa Review: "On the Possible Death of Monsieur Smith," "My
    Suicide Returns to Me Each Year," "The Year John Cage Was Born"
Ironwood: "Clarity: A Knife"
Literary Review: "Nine Times the Space," "Two Stories"
Malahat Review: "Fat Lady"
Midway Review: "The Front"
Negative Capability: "Prison Guard"
Nit & Wit: "Finishing Touches," "Nude Descending a Poem"
Ohio Journal: "Aftermath: A Way of Counting," "Notes Toward My First
    Russian Novel"
Piedmont Literary Review: "Hunger"
Plains Poetry Journal: "Victims"
Poetry Now: "The Hagiologist"
Poetry Wales: "A Drowning Man Is Never Tall Enough"
Poets On: "Parthenogenesis," "The Survivor Does Not Go Away"
Proof Rock: A portion of "Surrogate Dancer for the Man with No Legs"
Shenandoah: A portion of "Surrogate Dancer for the Man with No
    Legs"
Southern Humanities Review: "Another Russian Novel: Fragment"
Stone Country: "Subsong"
Trees: A portion of "Surrogate Dancer for the Man with No Legs"

A
Hunger
to Sustain
Us

Beyond a certain point there is no
return. This point has to be reached.

FRANZ KAFKA

Surrogate Dancer
for the Man with No Legs

Being born means looking for your
name, finding it means you are dying.
EDMOND JABÈS

What a fool, this man who keeps a cemetery in his pocket.
He is going   back   to turn   on the lights   inside
a burning   house.   A woman   from the
library comes to   read   to   me   on   Tuesdays.

Birdlike,   she opens   her briefcase,
stacks the books on   the table   before   her.
She   thinks   I'm   blind.   Her face
is chalkdust   and pretty;   her   legs

postmarked with   veins,   blue   with doodles,
parted.   See?   She reads from Tobit   the
warnings of sparrows, reads something   about   Gaza,
the blaze   of the noon.

"I'm   not   blind,"   I   would   tell   her.   "I
have   no   legs,"   I'd   say.
How   can   I   disappoint   her?
I   ask   her to dance while she   teaches

me braille.   A   prayer   book   cracks
shut. A   man   goes   out when   the   ice
is purple;   his
ankles   ache.   A beaver   all   night   has

chewed   at   his   pants.   He
arranges to take   smaller   steps.   His eyes

3

adjust to the   cold, burrow   inside   bluish mounds.
I   can   feel the difference: the

heft of   the eye   when it   sees,   the
weightless eye   when   it   doesn't.   A
woman from the library   comes   to
read   to me   on   Tuesdays.

I ask   her to dance.   This is   a
season   we   have no name   for.
It fills   us with anger   and   doubt.
It is   a time   for   finding

our names.   Though   the thermometers   say
it is hot,   men   stick
to   the   metals   that   hang   from   their
necks,   freeze   to   gold-colored

watches.   This   is   a season   of old
men,   wisdom tied to the   tonsils,
hearts   dropping   out   of
the   body   without   any   warning;

a   season   of young women   cracking
eggs   in   a pan;   a season   of   voices, the
slitting   of a flour   sack,
the sigh of   dead   snow;   a season

of trees,   black   spruce and tamarack,
every   inch   of   the   sky   sifting
down   to the roots. This   season   is   white,
too   white   to   be   winter.   Still, it

is   carried   in   on spoons.
All year long   the sky   is

4

too   short;   everything   shows. No need
to rush   through something as intricate as the

weather.   Words are   getting   lost   inside
her.   Sick   rooms
are   logically pale, forgotten, torn away   like
tablet paper.   No one wants   to   remember

their smell: white and whispery,   something
like sleep,   something   like   a   priest's
breath   at a wedding.   The
names   on the   door

are   written   in   pencil;   the articles
on the night stand, once only   practical,   replaceable,
are   suddenly   blessed:
sticky   spoon,   slow   clock,   bud

of tissue.   Water   in the glass is kept at a certain,
gray level.   You discover   the point
of   the pulse: it is   there
to   be   taken. A man   looks at a map. Cities

smaller   than   buttons; rivers   motionless   and
blue,   dead veins   in   autumn.   I
keep   turning   down   the   wrong
world.   Globes

like   rich, lopsided women; old battle   maps
for   when   there is nothing   left
but God.   Road maps   in   glove
compartments   ride   the   raddled   borders,

scale   every   inch.   Maps
precise   as absence;   deserts so small

I'm   ashamed   to   die   of thirst.
"I'm   not blind," I   would   tell   her.

"I   have no legs,"   I'd say.
Such disappointment.   Failure   requires
a new suit with narrow pockets,   the threads
all running   one   way.   It   demands

the blunt   color of a toad.   Touching
bottom   is   an   occupation   for which   you
have to   dress.   Idle.   Time   to
count   the   faces of a crumb. The radio at   this depth:

knobs,   static,   voices   no bigger than buttonholes.
Tomorrow's   weather   gets   through.   A name.
                                                    My name.
What a fool, this woman who keeps a womb in her pocket,
a hollow house. She is going back to turn on the lights.

Hunger

Strange, I had words for dinner
Stranger, I had words for dinner
Stranger, strange, do you believe me?

JACK SPICER

She sits like a chandelier in a ship's ballroom.
Her tables set with oranges, rum, cakes
In the shape of Mediterranean islands.
I return from a country. She tells me
What food is, what pumice is.
I've forgotten everything. She sits with her legs
Crossed; her lap like a Japanese alter.
She tells me the meaning of horoscope,
Wedding, trapeze, orangutan, suggests articles
On fashion and finance. I try to explain.
I return from a country.
She arranges a list of people worth meeting
Now that I've arrived: a diplomat
With a candelabrum who traveled through Russia
On a freight train;
A countess blessed with the luxury
Of not being able to remain.
I require someone with a skinny tie,
Kafka in a dark suit marching through real snow drifts;
I need Balkan countries at my disposal;
I need lessons on a saxophone, knowledge of death
And other things. "She is an old lady
With grapes beneath her skin; she carries pictures
Of your mother wrapped in cellophane."
I've been gone a long time.
I bring rain. I bring hammers. I bring books.
I come from a country, and I bring words.
This is their word for chair, their word
For fountain, for succulent. I assure her:
We will find a hunger to sustain us.

The Year John Cage Was Born

The year John Cage was born, his father
Set a trap. For thirteen days, in a submarine
Of his own design, John Cage's father
Stayed submerged—for thirteen days,
With thirteen men, on Friday.
And when John Cage's father came up, he said,
"Well, John, top that." So a precedent was
Set that fathers and sons were expected
To follow. The challenge would be passed on.
Records in '48 were not so easily established.
My father's submarine was borrowed
And in need of paint. I'm not making
Excuses. The sunlight danced over the dent
On the bow. They came to the docks to see him
Off: a man carrying a sketch of the mayor,
A woman in a floppy hat. The picture
Of my mother shows her head slightly bent
As if she were listening to the bumble
Of a motor car speeding out of sight. The white
Ribbon in her hair sags like a cripple's
Shoe lace. The conversation centers on how cold
It will be, on how hot. The one thing
For certain is that there will be discomfort.
There will be times when breathing
Will have to wait. They barely look at one
Another, my father on the deck, my mother on the
Dock, straightening the ribbon in her brown hair, as
Everything around them, for one moment, stays afloat.

Victims

I pretend the count is accurate.
It isn't. A leg gets counted twice.
A throat or two misplaced botches up the total.
And I must count again.
Or guess. There is the problem
Of imposters: a fingerprint, oval, lost;
A tooth that doesn't fit.
The victims of mine disasters make it easy.
Solitude refines them.
Their final breath sweetens
With the darkness and the coal.
Bottled up, they stay the way they are
Longer than I want them.
I drag them out like silverware,
Blue in slender rain;
I lay them lengthwise, heavier than I want them,
Alphabetically arranged.

Hard Evidence

I prefer the unknown.

JACK SPICER

At this depth things hold on tighter,
Don't let go of what they are. Ten below.
The trees, skeletal, rigid with fact.
Birds drop their hands inside their pockets.
In hotel rooms I find it more difficult
To conceal my body. The moon at the window;
The increments of ice on the ledge;
A poker chip slides down the back of Chicago.
Winter has a false bottom: twenty below.
Things don't remain the same.
I'm reading Kierkegaard or Arthur Conan Doyle.
I become a distant relative, hard and white,
Against my former throat. In the park,
Birds flap out of the benches: wings bend
Like the brims of gangster's hats.
In hotel lobbies I locate evidence:
The ashes in the plates, the mirror
About to thaw, the mystery intact in every clue.

My Suicide Returns to Me Each Year

My suicide returns to me each year
Bearing less and less resemblance.
He is fat with rumors. My suicide
Is laughable and fat, mumbles
Latin into a cramped hole.
Over anything that doesn't move
He pauses, moves and then reflects, thin as doubt.
"Fool," I say. My suicide returns.
He doesn't know me. He says he has learned
The ingredients. "Idiot," I say.
Fat with what he does not eat,
He moves beneath his movements, gestures
From within. I identify myself
By falling through the slot.
Without my thinking it is winter, it is winter.
All by itself it will be spring.

On the Possible Death of Monsieur Smith

He's been trying to tell me he's died. The evidence
Came in for years, but I ignored it. He lined
His office walls with burial jars from Egypt.
I examine his memos for clues of his demise:
Requiems for a clavichord he composed in secret,
Passages from a Tibetan book he copied during
Lunch. His habits confirm this: his desk faces
The west; a tile removed from the roof is kept
In a locked drawer. I explore the odds
And the ends, his jump to conclusion, the dum-de-dum
Of ledgers written in red ochre. I speak
To his possible widow about his possible demise. It
Lets him do the things he does so well unnoticed.

The Hagiologist

Scissored by uncertainty, my woman tells
Me all is surprise. Saints, unfortunately, aren't
Very good with holy things. Details of that
Conversation elude me. So many. The butterfly
Becomes the flight of a conquered city. The sun
Is getting started in the east. There are
A few things on which we can rely: the border
Has no country on either side. Abstract, you see,
Blind like a stuffed sock, this is my
Reassurance: before there was God, there was
Someone who looked like him. I should have
Been more attentive, taken her hand, smelled it,
Tasted its presence up to the wrist, listened
To her complicated description of the birds
While the birds clipped out the sky.

The Front

I lost my father's war, its cities,
Its general plan, its movement on the map.
The losses are marked with blue pins:
London misplaced at midnight; Stalingrad,
Dresden gone; Hiroshima, a hole dropped
Inside another hole. I can't identify
A single victim
Wrapped inside his own hands.
I lost the part where barbed wire
Was knitted into nations; I lost
The language. The word Treblinka:
The breaking of thin glass.

Things to Be Afraid Of

Light. The cities' aortas of light.
Things to be afraid of: nowhere
And platitudes. White places.
And places to dance. Apocalyptic
Ceremonies when we find the language
For them. Nothing. To be afraid. There is
Silence and words. The breaking leaves.
The effortless. Schools of white
Butterflies, like schooners, like bits
Of torn paper. There is nothing. Our names.
Pictures of a beautiful woman
Touching the eyes of a yellow dying
Man. Things to be afraid of.
Plagiary. The planes of air. Anything
Permanent. The breakable. Winter,
Charts, spare rooms, matches, songs
Nailed to the chest. Anecdotes.
Manganese and mythology. Extra
Innings. Enumerations. Always
Nothing which is nothing to be afraid of.

Fire in the Dance Studio

The excursion is the same when you go
looking for your sorrow as when you go
looking for your joy.

EUDORA WELTY

All that year men listened to the radio.
Women with black gloves boarded trains
To anywhere. Their insides were sweet
With rust and mystery. We played pinochle
And gin rummy, the face cards slapped
Down like barn doors. All that same year,
The hunter's boots, like tree stumps,
Grew next to the radiators. This is how
We came to the end of astonishment.

My sister dreamed of dancing in South
America. Her twirling blue skirts shimmered
Like a pilot light as she danced in front
Of the huge mirrors where revolutionaries
And priests took the same vows, where
The dictator wore his road of ribbons.
She remembers the fire, the way it danced
In her slippers. I remember the glass
Blower, a curve of glass fish when he

Was calm, a pelican when he was sleeping.
Rage filled the room with litter: yellow
Mice and tiny dolls, a twist of arms, cuts
Of inclement weather. Love would leave
His breathing exquisite, like the bluish
Space in a bluish bottle. Doubt would put cracks
In where they ultimately belonged. I don't want

To feel anything: the day-spin of emotion
Stands still, holds on like dust. He would

Breathe empty, heavy spaces. "Are you
Alone?" he'd ask his wife while she'd
Exhale children. In the chill of his latest
Creation, the only possible answer was yes.
And he couldn't hear it. My mother
Wipes away the borders with her back
And forth hand. When she polishes
The foreign coins, she neglects to mention
That they can't be spent in any country

But the one her husband plunders.
And still it's an easy mistake to make.
Through the blue light of the blue
Afternoon, my mother chases cobwebs,
Oriental cities just before the soldiers
Take home the streets. When a poet's
Mother goes senile she says, "The moth
Is waiting at the top of the stair."
She too dreams of South America,

Of dancing among graves with gray-haired
Poets, of European ships sinking off the shores
Of Argentina with their cargo of sabers
And flowers and cruets. The exotic
Birds hang in the trees, clack like painted
Tin snips until everything grows quiet.
The old man sits on his porch, remembering
When his spit was still silver. Señor de nada.
In the abandoned opera, the violins are

Strung with cobwebs. While mules rock
With the silver from Bolivian mines, twin-engine

Planes spin out over the mountains. This
Is the drop-off of dreams. Look as linking.
Look as action. I look both ways . . . between
Metamorphosis and mutation.
The dancer in an imaginary dance must
Carefully dance so as not to disrupt the
Event or become a part of the event

She is disrupting. How much of her is
Silence when she brushes out her hair?
Still we are asked to imagine and not
Imagine her, the splatter of that hair
Upon her shoulder. We detect in her wavering
Presence the presence of another, the way
Pluto was discovered in the motions of
Uranus. In spite of ourselves we see
To the other side of ourselves: such beautiful

Imaginary poplars near such splendid imaginary
Ponds. I listen. "The moth is waiting
At the top of the stair." With every
Name in the book I name. Words. The
Edgewise words, puzzles of the heart. The
Yes. The no. The yes. Cider-colored
Leaves drop through September. There is
A wedding. My sister is there. The sumac
Carries its red candle. The first snap

Of rain. The trees bend with it, bless
With it, carry it like priests. The stained
Glass of autumn crashes all around. Fire.
The tango and the waltz perish. The enormous
Mirrors shatter. The fox-trot dies, dizzy
And spinning. The senses frozen into jewelry,
There is no way of knowing. No one says,
"I can't wait for the ending." The destination,
Once perfectly imagined, is already behind us.

Losing
the Word
Imaginary,
the Word
Real

What is spoken is never, and in
no language, what is said.
MARTIN HEIDEGGER

Nude Descending a Poem

The nude descending a poem is not a nude
Descending a stair. Her desires are different;
Her hair, less disheveled. She persists
In uncertainty. Men may argue
About the color of her eye, its dark insistence,
Its eventual meaning. The figure of her flesh
Is not the figure of her descent. The nude
Descending a poem is not a word; she is not
The reach of the word "light" through the word
"Window"; she is not the reach of the thigh or the dark
Vowels of her breasts. Her hair in the shape
Of its color, its critic, she adjusts
A complicated pin on her otherwise uncomplicated
Clothes. Her window carries a formula for light.

Two Stories

As soon as there is only myself
there is nobody.

PAUL VALÉRY

Valéry insists that in building a locomotive
It is indispensable for the builder
To work at eighty miles an hour. Valéry
Once sat in the Paris Métro

During the German occupation; immune to all
Around him, certain of the speed
Of his creation, he imagined daisies in a dented
Pail. The speed accelerates or diminishes

According to the task.
On a bench with a ballet poster blazing
Around him, the color pink spreading
Off a wheel, Valéry works with his allowance

Of light. "Daisies in a dented pail."
The train to Montmartre is full of soldiers
Hanging from the hand straps. Loud, they light
Their cigarettes off the girl's yellow bonnet

They are burning on the floor.

Stone Music

I lost the word frenzy, the word goldfish,
The word plum. The Papuan tribe knew
How to create a shrine of the language.
When someone died they would ban the use
Of certain words that named objects
Or characteristics of the member who had died.
A language with loss built into it.

My latest fear is based on something real.
It's not that I'm like Strindberg striking
The air with a knife at imaginary foes.
I've lost the word imaginary, the word real.
Sometimes it is as if I drag the air around

Behind me. My language is growing smaller and
Smaller. Once I stood in Martello Tower
Where Joyce began to write *Ulysses*. Birds dropped
Through that sky like broken scissors. Renew

The battle. Snap back. That tower was built
To turn Napoleon around. The clipper ships
Like candelabras jacked high up on the sea.
Then it turned me back. The water buckled,
Tumbled, lathered on the stones. The wind cut
Short. The sky blew shut over the late
Afternoon, ended on the word urgency.

Oboe, bride, and body gone, the air full
Of the moment. The ullage of language.

Then there is the dream of fathers, the dark
Chroniclers. I am rolling a word around

With my tongue: Door. Seed. Shadow.
I say the word mother, and it is like leaving
My breath on a window. If only I hadn't
Grown tired of the sea. I consult

The notes of Michelangelo. Net. Cane. Paper.
What were the old formulas? Try first
With sheets from the Chancery. Boards of fir
Lashed in below. Fustian. Taffeta. Thread.
Paper so thin the writing falls through.
I lost the word pearl, flint, exquisite.
I was trying to explain the virtues

Of accessibility. Find some object that will speak
The lessons of the ordinary. Where is the world
When you need it? The planet rolling along
In its groove: the air eroding it, polishing it,
Wearing away the mountains, even the waves
Of the ocean rubbed off, the pine forests
And the rain forests sanded away
In this friction. My mind once ovoid,
Now round, rolling. When I lose the word

Surface, I have nothing to hold onto.
I am afraid of widths, entanglements, and light.
What wizardry I deny, these exemplars
Of the irrational, templates of loss, the bees
Returning to their tabernacles. I am losing

The word febrile, caprice—the fiction
Of the self. It is as if a painter
Were losing colors, the sluggish grays,
The freezing blues, lilac, lake, and snow,
Until in the end his paintings resemble glass.

Even time is not chronological. At night
I am back in the wards, listening, listening.

Words. Words. Words. Thresholds into what
Is there. Brightly painted walls. Configurations.
Imaginings. The proper affirmations.
The capacity to enchant. Words. Words.

Suppose I lose all the words for birth:
Labyrinth and pulse. Or poem: a chandelier
Of sound, a rattling of light. Or nourishment.
I lost the word food while my wife
Was making sauce: crushed tomatoes, golden
Sherry, bay leaf. I keep talking

With my mouth full. My language depleted,
I need a word I can eat. When I stand
In the symmetry of being alone,
Ghosts mumble in the burning corners
Of the room. To my dismay there are things
That last forever. The waves. The reliable
Waves. The intricacy. The pattern. The blue
Gadgetry of heaven spins out along the sea.

Deprived of the Fourteenth Century

I wake them in rooms
No bigger than bread;

I dress them
In sandals and hoods,
Bind them

With cord, give them carts.
Monks

Like ink pots, monks
Burning the noon
Oil. First learn

The blind side of things:
The high spots

Melting in the spring.
They copy Latin, hold
The silences together

Between the pages of
A book: trees,

Seasons, star point, code.
I select the pain
I think will save them:

Eternity.
This time it lasts forever.

Propellers over Amsterdam

When I stand in front of my uncle's bed,
His hands tied to the rails, I'm not certain
He knows me though he remembers
Everything. The girl in Holland is old now;
My uncle says she's young. Her face
Presses against wet glass. She fumbles
In her west pocket for the keys.
At dusk propellers over Amsterdam, barely.
The expression of the world
Changes: autumn, like shellac, thin
And polished with its rain. Order takes
The place of significance. My uncle
Remembers the girl, the name of her saint's
Dance, her body being read
Like a foreign language, a loaf of silence
In a mother's hands. Upstairs
Elders play pitch for ludicrous stakes.
A woman watches like a picture
Of a woman watching
Card players. Her face wears nothing
Well. How many times we touch, barely,
Like old people lighting candles in a war.
I wear the uniforms of both sides. Safe
That way. Mobile. Invisible. The meat
Is measured; the napkin, folded like
A last letter. I feed my uncle liver
From a plastic fork. Remarkably the light
Recovers on this side of the curtains.
The painful admission: whatever is left
Is enough.

Fat Lady

The thin are terribly close to becoming
Infinite lines; it is as if Euclid were walking
In an idea of an orchard picking
An idea of a sumptuous pear. In the
Pocket-sized evening, thought consumes
Thought and leaves us something to think
About. Green is an arrangement
Between two colors. The lovers rattle
In the musicality of motion: I am the
String; you are the percussion, full
Of sound and plump noises. This is how
Pain looks when it has nothing to wear;
This is how life looks when it puts
On its glasses, when it crams its pockets
With its impossible hands. The thin
Are severe, logical. They walk the wire
Of the self; they are more brittle
Than the mathematics that governs ice.
Discover the mechanics of a rose being
A rose, of a spool becoming a spool.
You will lose yourself
In the low noon of desire and things;
Activities, internal and external, leap
In opposite directions. I have a desire
For desiring. That girl in the olive dress
With the terrible jewel sifts through these
Lines yearning for mobility and space,
For the glue drop of night on night,
For the bump of birds on roof peaks, for
The tattle of clocks in the gray-shingled houses
By the sea. In the trailer a fat lady

Sits on a stool, full and overflowing, a
Fathom or more. Bottom heavy
With the blossom of herself, she shakes
Off her clothes. Her breasts cling to her
Body like children with dark mouths.

Finishing Touches

So I said to myself—I'll paint
what I see.

GEORGIA O'KEEFE

Flashing Gauguins at me, my wife complains:
Her hands yellow with worry why did
I force them into blue; how did I fit that angle
Of darkness into her eye? I paint a bird in her
Hand. Stump of whiteness. We wake up
The stories behind it, the cherry fire that burns
In its eye. Perfect. Spiritual. It will only know
The sky through rumors. It has too many wings.
My wife complains: her nakedness is lost
In my nudes. That knee is not her; that hair,
Too green; that throat slants with someone else's thirst.

Fear

Hippocrates saw it in Nicanor,
Who trembled at the sound of flutes
At a banquet. My daughter Nicole
Is suddenly afraid of everything:
The train that clatters in back
Of our house, freezing rain, sleep,
Old Cornish prayers. She is afraid
That people will not be there when she
Turns around. I would like to tell
Her that this will end.

I have seen lists of phobias, always
Alphabetized and orderly—from acrophobia
To xenophobia—as if in this rational
Arrangement one could control the chaos.

What about the fear of lists?
What about the fear of snow
Or the fear of becoming transparent?
What about the fear of wonder?
Or the fear of the abstract?
The fear of language? The fear
Of success? And then there is the fear
Of time. The fear that we will
Never die. What about the fear

Of waking up in the past,
Maybe being seated at a banquet with Nicanor,
Listening to the bone flutes, the ivory
Flutes, the reed flutes, watching
Her clutch her narrow throat

As if she were being smothered?
What about the fear of waking up?

Then there was my grandmother
Who feared insects. During her last days
She demanded that we play Mozart
Again and again. And before she died
She imagined all kinds of bugs.
Beetles crawled in and out of her
Old black shoes. There were so many
Caterpillars she said she didn't need

To wear her slippers. Spiders stepped
Around her fingers, strolled on her throat.
Moths swallowed the light around her
Diamond, her window, her lamp.
A wasp tiptoed on her shoulder.
Before she died
She had no fears at all.

Clarity: A Knife

They settle on invisibility the way some men
Settle on a price. Farmers: men who are certain
Of their equipment, obstinate like crowbars. Sceptical
Men who sharpen their collars; men ready with a dent.
A drunk, sweeter than the breath of a bee. An occasional
Saint, eloquent, a voice thin like shellac, a man
With a purpose, a man whose reason for not being there
Is always beautifully stated. A woman who wants
To be painted by Lautrec; a woman with a handful
Of luxuriant pears; a woman slimmer
Than possibility, an empire burning its cities
To keep warm. Ultimately, the miraculous comes easy.
Contradications meet. An uncle is a knife
Who can carve a whistle from a man's throat.
An aunt, a knife in search of warm bread.

Aftermath: A Way of Counting

Disasters have a habit of turning up our town: an earthquake,
A tornado, a cave-in, a crash. A ship goes down
Like a chancellor's dinner. Fire lights up the liquor store;
Bottles pop; muscatel and Chivas Regal spill through
The colored glass. The church is under water: Christ
With his burgundy wounds; candles, stump-short
And murky. This is a time when miracles are worked
Backwards. We know why Hopkins carried his nuns in his arms
Like broken umbrellas. The cave-in at the pharmacy
Keeps us occupied for days digging through the dramamine
And valium. Things don't look good: sleeping pills
Piled on our shovels. Is anyone left? Our Pliny keeps the details;
Our Voltaire listens for the rumble in the steps of his Lisbon
Church. There is no house old enough to hold the world
Back. After determining what's solid, we go to our neighbors
To borrow a crack. New occupations: we're busy leaving
Something out. We keep writing until the dead are spotless.

The Survivor Does Not Go Away

I send him to pick up packages,
To make deliveries of ice.
He doesn't.
I tell him to find a hobby: hagiology,
Astronomy. "Be immersible," I advise.
He has nothing to do; he plops
In the doorway like a man cut down
For dinner. I leave train schedules in his pockets;
They stop in his hands.
He dresses to disappear but never to depart.
The scarf hangs from his neck
Like the arm of a dirty child.
When the snow is exact, he looks in the glass.
He will never go away from his hunger.
I tell him to write a poem which will not allow
Him to survive. Absence begins to suffice.
He makes a list of what is missing.

Nine Times the Space

Only connect.
E. M. FORSTER

My granduncle fell out of a plane
On his way to World War I,
Which at the time was not considered
Strange or inconsistent with the tempo
Of the age. A war with parts
That didn't fit: trenches, gas masks, horses
With a sense of humor. Reality was Picasso;
Da Vinci's drawings came into their prime.
Tannenberg. Verdun. Château-Thierry.
Europe had lyrics to die in. My granduncle
Took it seriously. They spotted him in October
Floating off the green coast of Miami,
His naval machinist's scarf scrambled in the sea,
His face like a dent in a hat.
December he died. My grandmother carries
The clipping. Owen Joseph Haney.
I admire the way dead men stick
To their names. My grandmother knows
What I mean. Still I can't share
Her certainties. How to distinguish
Evil from benign absurdity?
His thirteen hundred feet of falling:
The abundant world approaching
Through the thinnest air,
Coming closer. Closer

Prison Guard

Every time my father sees me he apologizes
For forgetting to make duplicates of his keys.
All the while he is intent on watching my hands.
It's all right, I explain. When he looks at a butterfly,
My father reaches for his thumbprint. The job did that;
It made him half certain he was only partially there.
Though retired, he still tells the stories:
The tricks played on him at head count,
The lengthy interrogations over missing spoons,
The flashlight he shot into bed clothes.
My father doesn't leave the trailer anymore.
From the same small window where the night tips in,
He watches. The book with the pictures helps
Him identify the things that he sees: a bird
Landing in a tree like a burglar's shoe,
A lilac, a marigold, an auto.
This way when we're together we have something
To say. But the points we arrive at aren't there.
And after I leave, he wipes what I've touched with a rag.

Odd, the Bride Stripped Bare
by Her Bachelors

In a glass factory I cut eighth-inch
Glass into old frames, work back into the hand
Mirrors the image of the owner's face. Chips
Of glass glisten on the green cloth
Of the cutting table. A trickle of diamonds.
A crown for a broken family. Great Britain
Once banned the importation of mirrors
So an Englishman wouldn't have to wake up
Looking like a German or an Italian
Or a Turk. Good idea. The city is dark
With insinuation, dark with plot,
With place. The distant look
And grow more distant. I remember the eyes
Of the old days, of those who got out.
Odd. It is not as if they suffer
But as if they watch
Their suffering. I know a story: a bride,
Her bachelors, the dwarf like the dark ages,
The child who had my hunger but not my thirst.
Its systems like secret countries with seams
Stirred by secret ships. A story
With a moral but no meaning. The things we learn
To live with keep us from learning how
To live. I work in a math that has only
Odd numbers. Like damage I'm done.
The windows at twilight are half city, half
Face. The woman's legs delicately widen. A dancer
On her back, careful, a crack, as if she balanced
On her toes a dish of chemicals.
And if a woman prays, bent like a peasant looking

For her husband in the snow, she bears
The moment when I am most alone. It's anachronistic:
Secrets weighted down inside her like a robber's
Sack of jewels someone's found and stuffed
With pebbles. The thin woman, a stream, a dinner
Of string, looks out to the dim image
Of the world through her half-evaporated face.
The night imports a star.
In the morning the seas deposit the cities
Back onto the shores; the quern
That grinds out midnight grinds out dawn.
I work in a language that only has words. The
World moves over the world on wheels of stone.

A
Drowning
Man
Is Never
Tall
Enough

In the destructive element immerse.
That is the way.

JOSEPH CONRAD

Subsong

The cardinal bursts red in the room.
A sprung trap. Velocity. Luculence.
Its terror ricochets. So this
Is the pursuit of the self
When the self isn't there. Where once
It tapped at its reflection in the
Bedroom glass, now it darts without
A purpose. With a little luck, it
Shoots back through the hole
That had been its body, squeezes
Back into the comfortable sky.
I clap the storm window to the frame.
I return from my experiment. In the tree
Where it sits, it opens up,
Like a slashed wrist, red, radiant.

Elagabalus, Roman Emperor, Trickster Too

Elagabalus, Roman Emperor, trickster too,
Inspired by Saturn swallowing the stone body
Of his son, would invite the seven fattest
Men in Rome to dinner, serving them food
Made of glass, marble, ivory, brick.
A stone soup. An incredible glass duck.

Rumors spread that Elagabalus was mad:
A man living in the blue forest of his own head,
Listening to a thin and hungry music,
Like the sound of starving cats.
For years this continued until there were
No fat men left. So he invited

Everyone else to what was promised to be
His most spectacular event. Waiters floated
Beneath their wavy reflections on the bottoms
Of the silver trays, piled with almonds
And grapes and plums. Roast peacock
And pomegranates. Pallets of jams. Nectar

From Chinese bees. Sunlight from Syria
Flickering over the tiles. The food fell
In avalanches from the tables. And when
They were finished, Elagabalus showered
His dinner guests with rose petals
That he had had his servants gathering

For weeks. Big seductive drops piled up
Around the ankles. The dinner guests could feel
The undertow beneath their togas; their

Pelvises began to drop. A red airslide.
A red snow that would not stop falling.
The dinner guests could feel them

Around their throats like pieces of flesh.
Elagabalus stood on his balcony, imperial
And mad with the aroma of roses.
The chamber was dream-filled. He thought
Of the fat men—how they grew heavy
And sad. At night he still heard

That scratching cat-like music
Of their souls. He stood on his balcony
Breathing the red air around him.

Parthenogenesis

I alone am nourished
by the great mother.

LAO-TZU

There are only two impossibilities: birth and death.
Consider the cecidomyian gall midges. The offspring
Fill the mother's entire body. To be born without
The benefit of a father they swarm inside her corridors,
Devour her from the inside until nothing of her remains.
Consider how we lay our poisoned flowers

At the foot of the sea and call out across it.
Consider our imagining. To have it out with death
So to speak: the meat of the heart,
The spine like a burning shoelace, the red light
Of the heart burned off and the white light
Of winter glaring. I claw a hole in my name.

I wait before the tree; I am my own father,
Sharpening a blade until it's blue. Mother,
I need a word that is a language,
A bird that is the sky. I watch. Your eyes,
Silvery; your breath rolls off. And so
I plot the surrender to radiance where I am

Incapable of separating breath from breathing,
Where the tree is a bird that has cracked, where
The sky is a bird that swallows birds
Whole, where the stone is a bird that has eaten
Too much. Consider my hunger, consider
It, as I eat my way toward light.

Eraser

A nihilist with a sense of humor,
Thick and pink, it looks like a part
Of our anatomies. Even the word star
Is blackened on its stump. It knows
The way one moment is displaced
By another. To discover the least,
The minimum, it imagines the last,
Approaches the word mountain without
A theory for mountains; it soaks up
The word rain without a concept for rain.
With all that it swallows, you would think
That it would grow into something colossal.
Instead it flakes off, dwindles to
A little lump, a shrivelled piece
Of fruit, a bud that's going bad.
The stars? The mountain? The rain?
Pink crumbs left behind as if there were a trail.

Is (Is Not)

Between nothing and everything there is nothing:
All the empty items that make up
The delicate accidents of our lives—the dolls
With scratched green eyes, the color blue.
And between nothing and everything there is
Everything: the silent, crooked TV antennae
Like the masts of ghost ships; the magician's
Handkerchief; the glass of water. I fill in
The gaps with confusion, revelation, with a lyrical
Mess. I try to say what might be said
Given the impossible. The colored scarves
Are drugged and drowsy, dwindle, disappoint.
What seemed miraculous was, after all,
Only miraculous. The dove that seemed
So shocking climbs out of the sky. The flaw
Is obvious. We only see that for which
We are looking: one slip of the handkerchief,
One emptied, empirical sleeve. Some relief.

Bird by Bird

Having nothing is easy; counting it is hard.
Thinking of a bird is also a bird—a type
At least. Ask Jung when he found
The bird he dreamed of dead in his back
Yard. The sky the thought-of-bird
Flies in is cramped. The brittle music
Of winter is almost here. That means
The rivers are migrating south; that means
The people in the terminals are thinking
They're already gone. But they'll wake
In the morning and find snow on the ground,
And they'll fill the crack that's always waiting
Beside their empty beds. Sometimes looking
Is enough to lose the urge to turn
The world into words, and sometimes
The thought-of-bird must feel its way
Through the crumbly dark and enter the
Cold crack of sky. Sometimes nothing
Is too much. Bird by bird the sky is leaving.

Thin Ice

A thin skin of ice
Forms on our pails. Here things
Get

Harder. The identical days
Go by us, skid
Like sunlight

On the chunk of a hat.
The dreams
Go out in our eyes. If
It's not one thing,

It's two, and so on.
Snow spreads on the roofs
Of the shacks.

The snow that has fallen
On the bald tire in the backyard
Is in the shape of a halo.

Watching the Sailboats

> I became more and more excited about how
> words which were the words that made what-
> ever I looked at look like itself were not
> the words that had in them any quality of
> description. This excited me very much at
> that time.
>
> GERTRUDE STEIN

Now where was I? Oh, yes. Each morning
I go out to see how much of the past
Still remains. I take my measurements;
I'm often surprised. I must keep learning

What I already know. Sometimes the sky
Is scuffed; sometimes it's smeared with clouds;
Sometimes there's drowsy fog; sometimes a dog
Sleeps in the rain. And always, each and

Each moment is a discovery of a place that has
To exist. Words. I pull a string with nothing
On the other end. The only weight I'm feeling
Is the endless, endless string. Shortly, I imagine,

The impossible will happen; it has become, I
Assert, a necessity. I never intentionally
Went out in search of an image of the
Self. No, I went out in autumn, and it

Was as if I were standing in front of a burning
Hotel: the petals of ash, the incredible colors,

The color of liquor, the color of a man
Who has settled on a few wounds. But as always

There is a merger of moments, and in the
Nick of time, time is saved. I lay
My abstractions on the top of a piano. Do
We really need a new religion to explain

The death of God? I feel queasy before
The quintessential, this crisscrossing mind.
Meanwhile, I look at the sailboats on the lake,
Huge artificial birds unable to lift themselves

Out of the weather. Sunfish and Bluenose slide
Through the light. It's the predictable that surprises
Me. The sails tip: the spillage of the main
Sails, the slivers of the jib sails. A ballet

Frozen on a postcard, white and red and
Yellow and blue, as beautiful as propaganda.
They move like clockplay. And always that question
Of time remains. Will it work? Will the wind

Conk out over the hotels and over the sails?
I pull the string, the endless string. Was that
What I was telling you: my discovery of that something
That always exists between now and now?

The Destructive Element

The nude sits in her chair with the cheap
Cloth cover, green and yellow, like a sloppy
Garden. What does Rembrandt see when he goes
For a walk: horses and boats, etc.? Once
You begin there is always the possibility you'll be
Unable to stop. And then as soon as one
Thing is described it becomes something else.
The pale, uncertain color of wheat changes
With the wind into the color of bees.
Try a landscape, a pitchfork angled
In a loaf of hay, a church with a grape-heavy
Bell. I grumble over the demise of blue.
When it's done, accomplished, nothing is altered,
And the space my body occupies is nothing
Else but me. Where is the line drawn
Between the man who suffers and the man
Who captures that suffering in swift, silent
Notations? We are back in Munch's painted
Sickrooms where his sister is still dying.
Hermetic. Sealed. The self slips through
The colors. I walk out into the smothered
Gardens. Everywhere I walk I clear
A space by spilling space. The inside
And outside touch. Creation takes time
By surprise. Another example: try a word
That will catch the condensation of blue
In her less than blue eyes. I is too lean
A word. Cézanne knew what he was doing
When he'd leave his empty canvas on a stone.
Or in the grass or on the shore. It would
Collect rain prints or the loosened shadow of a bird,

The skeletons of dying leaves, the flame
Of dying leaves. Finally, in a white room, a man
Lies in a white dream where he turns puzzles
Back into puzzles. If only the wine goblet
Would shatter. If only a woman, her bracelets
Spilling like fruit trees, would walk through
That door, carrying him as a child.
When the man in the white room, in the white
Dream, starts putting his life back
Together, he finds he's missing the holes.
Describe. Describe it. The clouds crumble
On the edge of the city. That's a starting
Point, an observation. The answer to the riddle
Is sky and river and tree. That's given.

World News

The liturgical drama of a mass society.
JEAN BAUDRILLARD

The dark persistence
of the voice. The water-clogged look.
We become what we
behold.
Underground water touches
the   roots,
the   buried cities,
touches the feet of the dead. I let
my head
be ripped
out from under this dream.
The smoke—I can't get it off me.
This is not   the world.
This is not.
We are being counted.
The dream worlds touch us.
The slavery. The circus.
These dark dream names:
Somoza, Amin, Pinochet.
Botha and Perón
are dining in my kitchen. Screams are made
of silver. These blazing
cities, Soweto, Beirut, Belfast erupt in my
living room.   The poor,
the homeless,
the starving children of everywhere
are huddled
in my den. It never gets easier
to watch

the dying mouth. We are being cured.
A light
is touching us. A talking light.
Che Guevara is buried
under the bed;
Lee Harvey Oswald
lives behind blue drapes.
The light says something in light.
Women are trying to find a language
for their own bodies.
Star Wars spins in my attic.

The air
shakes over my head
with victims.

A corporation
is dumping toxic waste under my couch.
I can't get the dreams
of generals   out of my nostrils.
I can't
get the smell of dead babies
out of the tan carpet.
An evangelist is stuck in my furnace.
Airplanes
are burning holes
in my windows.
All this living in light.

I can't get the
smell
of money   out of my hair.
In my basement with the broken
lacquered clock, with the pool table
and the cat hair,
a dolphin is dying.

A Drowning Man Is Never Tall Enough

Death was defiance. Death was an
attempt to communicate; people feeling
the impossibility of reaching the
centre which, mystically, evaded them;
closeness drew apart; rapture faded,
one was alone. There was an embrace
in death.

VIRGINIA WOOLF

I

I hear the squish, squish of shoes
As if someone were walking along
The bottom. The drowning man wears
No footprint. Strangeness always.
The tubes of fish thrown upon the shore,
I ignore the craft warnings,
The chiseled water, the dark slice
Of sails. All my lines down I tire
Of ingenuity. The dead
Fish, the stories of the sea written
With the broken pencils of their bones.
I once watched a retarded boy
Turn a button like a moon
Into a button hole. When he
Would go down to the lake, he would
Stuff his pockets and wear heavy shoes.
He would watch the fish, its big
Unintelligent eyes staring
As it thumped its life out against
The side of the boat. The eyes, hard
And small, the heads of black screws.
If we are going to be saved
Let us get it over with quickly.
I pull up anchor, like an aching tooth.

II

My father carries with him a terrible
Knowledge: words inevitably select
The wrong person to express their meaning.
Now my father writes these crazy stories
Where nothing happens. He says they are
About his life and wants me to read them.
Our lines snarled, we fish on a river.
Along the banks the birds straighten the cricks
In their unusual necks. Beneath us
Fish slip, their bodies like the handles
Of tarnished pots. A storm cloud churns; the water
Kinks. We are inside one of my father's
Stories entitled "Fear of Water."
I am reminded of Nietzsche in his
Impenetrable Turin writing
His impenetrable prose after
He watched the horse being beaten. "I would
Rather be a Basel professor than God."
Certainly. Even God would agree.
All day things drift by us: photographs
Of weddings; a gold watch, its chain
Trailing behind it; a hat. But there is
Something down there that won't come up. The snag.
I cut myself away. Later we hear
Someone has drowned. I keep looking for my
Father; he, wiser, keeps looking for me.

III

Leaner than wheat one day I arrive
Announcing my hobby: denial.
A woman plays the piano,
A gold and rickety music.

I leave the rivers running all night,
Enchanted by the waste, the isolated
Blue of waste. Leaving lives in our
Evaporating fictions; motion holds
Everything in place. One day I arrive,
Announcing my hobby. I am down
By the sea with the singer by the sea.
The sea teeters and turns, circles its own
Secret, the blossom of the self,
The dark onyx of the self.
It sings in the spin and the gimickry
Of what is created. The drowning
Man stands with dark sobs of oil
On his trousers, on the rag that he
Clutches. He says, "I do not use
The word love enough or use it once
Too often." As always, I leave
Something out: a reason, a plan,
An indispensable middle.
The retarded boy scoops up his
Reflection in the water
And presses it to his face.
My father stands in one of his
Own stories reaching for a word
He knows he'll have to erase: my name.
The voice of the singer by the sea
Turns into sky all around us.
It is summer; the beaches are
Glue golden. There is wakefulness
Even in the stones. The drowning
Man dreams of fish with small, black eyes.
The world stays the same, influenced
By the usual alchemy.
The curious birds, who tilt
And circle, seem never to touch the sky.

My First Russian Novel: Alien Language, Alien Things

Even when speaking of alien things, the poet speaks in his own language. To shed light on an alien world, he never resorts to an alien language, even though it might in fact be more adequate to that world. Whereas the writer of prose, by contrast—as we shall see—attempts to talk about even his *own* world in an alien language.

MIKHAIL BAKHTIN

Notes Toward My First Russian Novel

And we make of what we see, what we see clearly
And have seen, a place dependent on ourselves.

All her life she wanted to be a Russian
Novel, to take place in St. Petersburg,
To be a description of snow
Falling on an old man's shoes, a chuckle
Of rubles in his pockets. The long, white
Glove of moonlight floats down the Volga.

I am writing my first Russian novel;
Vaslov says that it is in no danger
Of being read. Freedom!

Claudine waits like a war bride, her dress
Curling in the wind, her heart swelling like a
Trunk in the czarina's bedroom. She can only
Think of Tolstoy's white bear—the game
He played with his brother—the wish
Will come true if you can stand in a corner
And not think of a white bear.

The white bear comes.

Does perfection involve consciousness?
Am anxiously awaiting a reply. Claudine loves
Old churches: the transparent fruit of
The windows, the powdery silence, the old
Man who sweeps after ceremonies.
He mends the broken fingers of the saints,
Polishes the wounds so they shine. Infinite

Care. I am sentimental: Claudine's mouth,
Rainy nights, candles, etc. How to begin?

Already I grow stale
Seeking my replacement. I require less and
Less. When I eat again it will be
Out of a sense of experimentation.
I can think of nothing but a white bear.
Lumbering through moonlight, dipping
His white paw in the trough.

An old woman with plans for the past,
Frayed at the edges, watches the street
From her window. Vaslov, black-eyed and lean,
Forgets about suicide. A woman in labor
Heaves like a church bell. The child's heart
Is packed, a bullet. Two men sit

In a Moscow bar. The light
Is slowly sipped from their table.
One searches for a perfect conclusion;
The other, for a perfect excuse.
I work hard at being nothing
But myself, at suspending myself

In others. For Claudine I include everything:
The rattle of the Trans-Siberian Railroad,
A carriage full of wounded from the Czecho-Slovak
Front. The nets hang from the gray fishermen's
Shacks on the Caspian Sea; violet hues
Attend the Ural Mountains; blocks of ice
Are stacked like hat boxes on the banks
Of the Neva River. I spend six glorious

Days describing Rasputin's face. Nothing
Makes sense without the most insignificant
Fact: I pass her a plate of roasted
Hare in a restaurant in Khiva. Black
Bread and vodka, smoked fish. I make it

Ten o'clock. We hear the guards
In the cellar unfastening the clasp
That holds up a girl's necklace. It falls

Like a dying wasp. Vaslov has given up the idea
Of revolution, philosophy, God. He tells
Claudine in secret, "Desperation is the only
Muse." She confesses: she loves D
Desperately. Who is D? The bite of weather:
January stiffens; early April plugged
With snow. I should have saved

For a time like this. Read more theology,
Increased my vocabulary, improved
The quality of something which at present
Is obscure. Her curiosity is cured. She
Hears the voice of her father, his heart
Clopping against his black chest, "So we are
Not to be taken anywhere?" I have lost

My ability to deceive: the device

Is my design. The earth, the green and gold
And russet earth is solved. February
Contracts; the entry of July is moist with
Acceptance. Everything comes true: the world
Separates into what is and is not her.
Suddenly flowers are named after her nipples, lace
Named after her flesh. The white
Bear? The white bear is missing. The white
Bear arrives. Something is wrong.
I have to ask: am I suffering?

Excerpts from My First Russian Novel

Now I depart
with flaming hair
As WE;
Not I

VELIMIR KHLEBNIKOV

"Her beauty will cause us great consternation"
"Sure I had my doubts"
"First there was that perpendicular pronoun"
"Now it is toppled" "I lost"
"My body" "Words" "freezing; her mouth" "around
The words" "The enormous intimacy"
"Mere" "words" "Mirror" "words"

"Insomniacs, I love you. I want you
For my own. I want you to stay up"
"Writing my poems" "for me"

"I will protect you"
"From wealth"
"Words" "around the words" "she touched"
"Look at the grave" "in my
Chest" "look at Chernoble" "look at the plum"
"Night"
"Oars are rising" "irrelevant rain"
"Irrelevant eyeball" "owls"

"Compromise"

"Lights are going out" "in great globs"
"Words" "her mouth" "wound around them"
"Bolsheviks" "catching fire in their beds"

"I want to touch" "the middle"
"Of you" "I want to touch God"
"I want to be at the center of my own cry"
"Smell the music"

"Words touching"

"Smell the maps bleeding" "the nicked sky" "I lost"
"The past becomes longer and longer"
"Smell the calculations"
"I am"
"You"
"Mouth" "touching" "words"
"The orchestra askew" "all the copper gleam"
"Snarls of sound"
"Death is tying its knot in our mouths"
"Her beauty" "All the thinking things"
"Nicked" "sacred"
"All this soaring in the sky of thought"
"The authority of want"
"Liquid" "labial" "believable"

"I will protect you" "From this"

"Peasants like a cloudburst" "a dead country"
"Who will be" "saved" "Constellated dreams"
"She has words for want, a mouth for it"
"Words"
"Black bees spinning around the heart"
"Pull the blue from want"
"Words" "touching" "words" "touching" "want"

Another Russian Novel: Fragment

We have made it very clear that 20th Century man is dragging
around a thousand-year-old corpse (the past), doubled over like an
ant trying to move a log.

VELIMIR KHLEBNIKOV

In the story everything she does is symbolic:
The bird she has perch on her wrist, the long
Gown, the short smile. The courier is two days

Late. That's the way things happen in this story.
It adds to the suspense. And in the story we
Learn with great difficulty to call the river

Babushka (Grandmother). We read Gogol
In the dark; we sing Bolshevik songs over bear
Meat. In the story the woman's son becomes

A symbol as she holds him on her lap. She stares
Out to the turquoise mountains from her droshky.
She stares at all that is incapable of dying.

That's part of the theme. In the story there are
Always lovers who cannot love, peasants who creak,
Rivers that lean toward the sea, mountains

That disappear for several days. (Reality is not
Realistic.) The woman in the story decides not to be
A part of her own life. Her son lives without

Her; his life grows as steady as a chess master's
Eyes. Sometimes he listens in the Moscow streets
For the clump in a cripple's shoe, something

To remind him of his own humanity, his own
Vulnerability. He tries to imagine his mother, the symbol
She became, the crisp, fierce, imperial look

In her eye when the courier did not arrive
With the meaning of it all. The story has other
Endings but this will have to do: It is winter,

The rivers stop, the roads cannot find their way back.

Not a Russian Novel

> Language thus assumes a sovereign
> position; it comes to us from elsewhere,
> from a place of which no one can speak.
>
> MICHEL FOUCAULT

Moscow's winter fairs on ice: children
With snow in their hair, touching.
At Easter time peasants carve bread
On the graves of their ancestors.

Isn't this where the present should be?
His wife and his children must watch him
Go crazy, and deny that he's there.
He has time to study time—the inches
Of it. In college he studied Russian history.
Now a business man in a sad suit.

Askew. Serfs tote the city of St. Petersburg
In their aprons and woolen caps. He is leaving
His wife, his two children. The light
Of Moscow is burning in Napoleon's pupils.
Isn't this where the present should be?

Intimate. Blue.
Oh, the Winter Palace of Petrograd. And the logic
Of it—simply change the name
Of a city and everything alters: a lover's breath,

The weight of mirrors, recent inventions
Will suddenly vanish. He sits in the solarium
Clicking checkers. Oh, the chimney fires
In Trotsky's mad eyes. Visiting hours

Are scary. The scorched earth. The eyes.
A woman with chilly hair. A boy who keeps

A journal in a secret language. Everything
That isn't moveable burns. A terrible courage.
He lies awake listening to the nurses
Counting pills into those tiny crenelated

Cups. Bridges: Ash. Fields of grain
Turning into smoke. The aureole of burning
Barns and factories. The couple huddle together
As they walk away. Chagall's lovers drifting
In blue air. The flying fish, the chickens,
The rusty goats, the motherly cow. And Christ

In his white crucifixion, floating up there
Like God. The burning burning.
A massive failure of the imagination.
The arcanum of the self. The couple in black
Coats hold each other tightly so they
Disappear. The clouds, thick, majestic,
Plug up the sky.

My Life as a Russian Novelist

> To amputate literature from the individual!
>
> ROLAND BARTHES

        the house of my childhood,
The trees holding the evening in place.
Or the trees balancing the dawn.

She writes letters to my protagonists:
        Dear Yuri, Help me understand.
One thing leads to another, but not this.
It is fall. The trees have insomnia.
A white rope of smoke twists
Into the sky. Not this.

        something dark and dangerous
Is waiting on the other side
Of us. Luckily we don't look.

My lovers:
        the world entering me through their eyes.
My casual suicide attempts:
The cries of the world around me and glass.
        both jagged.

All that metaphysical dalliance.

        meanings.
How the expectations didn't really matter.

Dear Yuri,
I don't understand what is happening.

I don't understand what you're saying at all.
But I suspect, as always, that it is the truth.

     she wants dates, specific points of time,
Pin pricks.

When I believed and when I didn't.
I thought everything, everything in the world,
Was nailed in place, even the water
That really didn't go anywhere
     beside the house I was born in.

My eyes are going soft. I can almost put
My fingers right through them.

I drew the language
Out of me—
     in shreds—
Until it was
Something foreign.

I could make a list of all the places I never saw,
And say I was only saying her name.
Exhaustion. Exhilaration. The arc of the sky. An accounting
Of it all. A gathering up. A falling away.

Yes. Yes. Yes: I find my body every morning
Where I put it the night before,
But the mind, that's the hard part.

I watch her wishing herself in and out
     of the story of her life.

Dear Yuri,
I am dying
To know.

The sky swallows whole seasons: whites and
Greens, crimsons and a blue that has fallen
    out of the mind. Give us
The understood, the comfortable. But there is
Always the unfinished business
Of who I am.

    she wants it to mean something.
I understand that and it hurts.
In the spring the trees have to remember
    it all again: the green green green.

Translations of the Russian Novel

> For what you take to be a shattering of
> language is really a shattering of the
> body, and the immediate surroundings get
> it smack on the chin.

JULIA KRISTEVA

lyrics and icicles passages through
silence I will die for my doubts
haunted a stone locked up at night
the seeds of the season white
touch this round silence the vernacular
sweeping across wreckages the stain
on the butterflies' wings oblong the
lack a stump of water sun
falling into the air a cut in a
cup speaks the lake shakes mildly
its politics in life we never
quite made it up to the present
we are proposed then crystalized
in the tyranny of the past the
exhausted river the stone river
poisoned sleep we still believe in
the present the power to melt
words that universal music I'm
held inside my life shredded
moonlight still I risk becoming
a bridge sweet nuptial the
maternal body shattering into a
language I walk into the undulating
colors of her mind can anyone
forget the nocturnal smell of burst
water the things we once called to
sink into their new names water
lily bloodstone nail throat

The Meaning of the Russian Novel

And to go write-on-living?

JACQUES DERRIDA

One theory says the universe,
Once it has filled itself up
Having finished its blossoming,
Its homemade bomb, will collapse,
And time will run backwards,
Chasing itself back through itself.

Inventions will recede into the inventors'
Imaginations. Honey will turn into delusive
Bees. Cities grow smaller, buildings
Back up into blueprints. Crumbs become
Loaves and loaves become
Fields and fields become seeds. Pushkin

Is unwriting his worlds. Radios
In scooped out corners erase some
Wars. Rivers turn into clouds.
A farmer's duty is to take the world
Back into the ground.

Weddings unwind. Stumps blossom.
Milk reenters the breast; sperm
Jumps back into the penis. Everybody wonders
When the world will begin.
Cures lead to diseases.
Into our hearts fall the stars.

Children must unlearn the names of rivers
And the staggering rivers must forget the names

Of continents and the names of the stars.
When the children open
Their mouths, we hear the shattering
Of the world. We have tremendous

Guilt for things that will happen
In the future. With curiosity and pleasure
We recklessly anticipate
The time when we will be virgins.

Sometimes we sit and wait for everything
To thaw, for the unpollination, for
The falling away, the pure,
The first and final closing up.

The white bear walks back into
The blossoms of fog. Nabokov
Is remembering tomorrow.

Words burn up along the lines of the poem.
We live as if there were no yesterday.

The bullet leaves Mayakovsky's flesh,
The hole first sealed over with smoke.
Yesenin unwrites his blood poem. Marina,
Beautiful Marina, comes down from her
Rope, her private gallows,
Her hair twisted, her eyes twisted

Into clarity. Such precise pain.
Light minded.

Mirror minded. Everyone
Puts on his parachute
Before rising in the sky.

My Last First Russian Novel

The final belief is to believe in a
fiction, which you know to be a fiction,
there being nothing else, the exquisite
truth is to know that it is a fiction and
that you believe in it willingly.

WALLACE STEVENS

My mother spoke in a foreign language:
A cloudburst of vowels. The consonants
Crumbling. I see the window that her words
Would make: stained with her breath.

"If only I didn't have my life
To live over," Vaslov says.
And I tend to believe him,
His desires, his avalanche of desires,
His endless absence. Sometimes I say,
"Vaslov, let it go. It will be better.
I promise." And then Claudine
Confesses.

Subjectivity: the mirror gone dry.

We invented a language for the stone
Violin full of sadness, for the groaning
And the cutting
Sounds, for the violence

And the rain.
We would point to the stars and

Make sounds like glass
Scraping over skin. We ate

Smoked cheese, slices of lamb, kebab
Of mutton, vapor.
No one understands. I am thinking
Of tearing things out of the earth.
Radishes. Carrots. Turnips. Roots.

Coffins. Old rocks. The hard
Of hearing. Languages written
On stone. Intimacy. Cups. Scandal.

The moon is broken off against the window.
Liquor, sunlight, ennui.
I never know what moves down through me.
I don't carry the map of me anymore.
With her new language she would
Make love to the ear. Her breasts

Beneath my hands.
The moist territory in her eye.

She dreams of the Virgin—
A whole night of bright dreams
Inside her like bait, broken
And beautiful. Siberia bursts open
And ballerinas spin out.

One thing for certain: God exaggerates.

I am thinking of tearing things
Out of the sky. A crisis.

Khrushchev is watching a dead
Person walk past his window.

(Rumi explains that we are bowls

Of water and as we live we are
Being filled up until we sink below
The surface. That is death: inner water
Becoming outer water, merging.
That is also life.)

Claudine has two birthmarks.
She says it is because she was born

Twice. She would listen to Tchaikovsky's
Piano Concerto No. 1 floating through
The Wedding Palace
Until it got stuck in her hair.
I look into the berry of her eye.
Its gleam, its poison.
Naked men are swimming around her ankles,
Their genitals brushing against her ankles.

Each word is a silvery cave inside itself:
Language creating the self—
The white apocalyptic voice—
The crystal liquid of her sex.
A man is looking for his face. A child's
Severed arm reaches back toward her.
A handcuffed corpse is being dragged to justice.

Sometimes I say, "Forget the questions."
But I know that's all we have left.
That and a little laughter. Everything
Is sliced open like a beautiful day.

We can smell music and pain—sometimes amnesia,
Holy Russia and hallucinatory Russia,
Irreality and delight.
The future is ancient.

Pushkin said:
Red'ka!
Tykva!
Koby'la!
Repa!
Baba!
Kasa!
Kasa!

The nightingale's song killed itself.
This is the age when fathers die
And go zoom in the night air.

(Claudine when she dies
Will say the word window.)

Our thirsts touch.
Lenin's lean eyes look. The rock
Kremlins. A dead person with a suitcase
Walking by his window. I am thinking
Of tearing things out of the newspaper.
(The church has counted 21,000
Claimed sightings of the Virgin.)
(There have been 4,000 languages on earth.)
I am thinking of tearing things
Out of the day, out of my memory.
I am thinking of tearing
Things out of me.

Claudine's beauty turns into a great constellation.
I can never look long enough

At her looking. My I is on her eye.
I inhabit a curved space. No more duality.
The physical and conceptual dissolve,
The self absorbed in the other, buried
In blue.

A mouth takes back all words.
I am listening to the language
Of the maternal body. Trust
Me: this will have to mean
Nothing for awhile.

The Contemporary Poetry Series

Edited by Paul Zimmer

The Contemporary Poetry Series

Edited by Bin Ramke